CORRIENNE'S PHOENIX

CORRIENNE'S PHOENIX

A COLLECTION OF POEMS

J.T. MCKENNA

Copyright © 2011 by J.T.MCKENNA.

ISBN	Softcover	978-1-4653-5459-4
	Ebook	978-1-4653-5458-7

All rights reserved. No part of this book may be reproduced or transmitted in any form or by any means, electronic or mechanical, including photocopying, recording, or by any information storage and retrieval system, without permission in writing from the copyright owner.

To order additional copies of this book, contact:
Xlibris Corporation
0-800-644-6988
www.xlibrispublishing.co.uk
Orders@xlibrispublishing.co.uk

Contents

Dear Phoenix 7
A Dear Alliance 8
Born 9
Born Again 11
Burden 12
Catastrophic Conspiracy 13
Delivered Today 14
Exemption 16
Exit the Cage of Sin 17
GOD's Parchment 18
God's Words #2 19
Good Fight 21
Got Back 22
Heavy Hearts 24
I Can Be Free 25
Judgement 26
Love Endurance 27
Love is a Battlefield 28
Lover's Lost 29
My Dog 30
My GOD 31
My Sister, My Friend 32
My Temptress Dismay (My Mistress) 33
Negative Hope 34
Octroyed 35
One True Star 36
Only Holy 37
Personified 38
Pushed 39
Questions of Worry 41
Reluctant Idiom of a Loser 42
SALVATION! 43
Small Dreams 44
That Will Be The Day 45

That; Smells so Swell.. 46
The Arrival on the Caramel Sands.. 47
The Journey.. 48
The Toilet Paper which has Charisma.. 49
The Truth about Lies 50
The Wrong.. 51
Tongues... 52
UNFAIRLY CONVICTED!... 53
Worthless.. 54
Deceit at Its Best.. 56
Dreadful Eyes 57
Irish Luck... 58
Seductive, Sensuous. 59
The Best Contender... 60
The Lion... 61
The Practicality of Living Life 62

Dear Phoenix

Dear Phoenix, I Just want you to know.
That when you grow;
from young to Old,
your wings may spread.
Large and wide, strong and bold-
with a colour so vibrantly red.

Dear Phoenix, If you should ever frazzle
you need to know you're never too young to go.
So when you're old and weary.
Get yourself together, You've a crowd to Dazzle.

With a burst of exuberance and awe a plenty.
You're never to Old, to Start a fresh.

Dear Phoenix, Oh! How it is Lovely to see you again.
Dear Phoenix, Oh! How you really woo the men.
Dear Phoenix, I can't wait to see your show again.

Dear Phoenix, If I should ever fall.
can you teach me, how to dazzle them all.

Dear Phoenix, When I grow old,
I want to be just like you
Subtle and Swift, strong and bold.
And I will ask you, what to do.

Dear Phoenix, It's Lovely to see you again!

A Dear Alliance

Thank you, for helping me turn my world around.
When I Needed someone,
You were there, to pick me up and off the ground.
Yet I still feel Undone.
To my amazement, It was a surprise.
When I came to see what this:
could turn out to be like, I returned with a prize.
A friend, and a learning,
That not all things come to an end, Sometimes
we have to look within
to find the answers, of all our times.

Now a friend, we are
we have a connection
that keeps us, Not far.
It feels like an infinite
of Love, and Affection,
and we both know what's right,
It's a strong Limit of Protection.

Can I hold this for life.
When I struggle, I look up,
bless myself that I have a friend
like you, that can help me Strive.

Like a root of a Sprouting seed,
A new burst of life.
I as your first breath of Fresh air.
Is all that you will ever need.

Born

I wasn't born to fly;
but if I had too;
I'd do it, just so I could see you.

I'm going to live my life
struggle and strife
just so I can say,
you are the reason, for the way;
that I am here today.

I wasn't born to swim
but if I had too;
I'd dive right in,
just so I could see you.

I'm going to turn out good,
laugh at all those who are rude;
and cry for those, who deserve a tear.
I only wanted for it, that you were here.

I wasn't born to die,
but if I had too;
I'd die with pride
not needing to hide,
just because I knew
I'd be seeing you.

I wasn't born to envy
but if I had too;
I'd not envy, not any.

I'm going to be strong;
holding my head high,
even if I am wrong;
and no, I will never cry.

I was born to see;
I was born to be;
I was born for the victory;
I was born to just be me.

Born Again

Hail, preacher teacher.
Our pastor Peter.
With no other word; yet sweeter.
"You are born-again so are Christian;
you cannot be both Christian;
and born again-
they mean the same."

So I am;
but a humble servant to you;
Lord so Holy.

I fail to please you so fall under category;
a Sinner; but the father he redeems me; forgiven.
Thanking the Lord, and Our GOD.
For letting me live on.

Burden

Love each other and with that, carry burdens for either one.
Stand forth, beside each other, and never leave a job undone;
for the heavy hand of God, will stroke and magnify your burden
by it be upon you, this a sin,
God, will refer to you as a "give-it-in"

Manage, what can be managed, hurry what should be hurried.
Never drop a job, unless best: be it buried.
Moving softly through your day,
only worrying by what should be worried,
take up as and when it may.

For the jobs of God, are not the easiest but yet not the hardest.
Seek what best to be seeked
and whence your break become, break the bread
and drink from the cup, this wine;
Refer to it as my divine blood; Shining such a magnificent Red,
and with the bread, take and think of it as the bones of mine.

And for the reason only: "that God is with you"
Never hold a burden no more, Hallelu–

Catastrophic Conspiracy

This is a catastrophic conspiracy
When I was told, I was sworn to secrecy
Don't let anyone know about my son.
But that's not right, that's not fun.

So up with your rules; I'll do what I like.
I'll scream it from the rooftops-
I'll scream it on mic.
I'll party with it all night.
And you can think whatever you might.

Because I don't give; for your opinion is one.
I can go on all night laughing at you;
then our friendship will be done.
After that who will you have;
and what then will you do.

Don't let the world see your shades.
SORRY, shades—my colours are bright;
and that Is what I believe in. Too right!

But I'm going to party and scream;
about it from the top of the roof.
I'm sick of hiding and not being seen.
This is by far the best I've ever been.

Delivered Today

Lord has given me a home.
Lord has held me alone;
Divided from the world–
Leaving me to my own.

Lord shall deliver me friends;
with news on fold.
Lord be my friend;
take my hand and hold.

Carry me, my lord through it all.
Carry me, my lord; shall I fall.
Carry me, my lord; Cold and sore.
place me, my lord; my feet touched the floor.

Hard and trouble times, unfold.
But God be my strength–strong and bold.
God be my stone, my rock I shall stand.
God be my guidance, NOW! Take my hand.

Fallen from your support;
so high of the ground,
even when I fell;
the rush of air, made no sound.

I know I can trust you Lord.
O' Lord so strong;
to be there at the bottom,
the bottom of my world.

So here you be,
in your arms there is me.
Carry me, my lord back to the top.
Save me, my lord from what may be.

Strong I stay through day-by-day.
Here I stand, with news to say.
God; my lord has delivered me;
He has; delivered today.

Exemption

I cannot be more proud;
to stand within the crowd.
And be exempt so honourably,
fail to treat my family so;
makes me hate you so horribly.

God, you had your way with me;
I know the path of which it should be.
"The path of Righteousness;
is the choice that fits best."

Now I will help my Family without exception;
Deliver them unto you, and make them feel,
what I had felt, the Exemption.

Granting relief unto them, will make me Awe you more;
Granting friends with kindness, love and grace.
I will fall, fall and keep falling: until my knees–Shall meet the floor.
I will then say, you exempt us; with your loving embrace.

Exit the Cage of Sin

When you feel you're enclosed within.
Remember, Jesus is our virtue;
the open door, to a cage of Sin.
Pray, and Jesus shall redeem you.

Never fear you are trapped;
Jesus will come and be your saviour.
Satan's chains are forever snapped;
this was in God's favour.

In God's favour you were brought to him;
In God's honour he cleaned you of sin,
Jesus is the name I Love.
Jesus is the one I love.
Jesus is the one and only.
He makes me feel so holy.

GOD's Parchment

My word is only true.
because it comes straight from you
he writes what he wants to.
You're challenging me. O' lord;
Just say what it is you needed too.

Written in Admiration,
I feel as I am your total creation.
Quill and parchment,
Analysing every compartment;
You write what you need,
and you do it through me.

God, it's awesome, how you do.
You do it all the time-
How amazing it is too.
When I fail to Rhyme;
You sort that problem.

God you're good.
You abolish all that is rude.
God you're strong;
helping all that are wrong.
God you're Solid,
helping those who forbid.

You do it all.
As I say; I say again:
You will never, ever fall
He is Risen;
and Risen he has, through it all!

God's Words #2

I know you're the kind of man.
That would understand;
so I brought you here-
tonight my dear,
to give you my hand.

Now hold on tight;
I will try to make it right.
When we go up in the sky;
and look back down, from way up high.

You'll see something;
you've never dreamt of seeing.
Wonderful views from up here!
Wouldn't you agree; my dear?

So magnificent, an extravaganza.
Now I wonder—where your fans are.
Think of all the time we've had together.
Don't you just wish: that, that was forever.

I must bring it up; as it has pondered me.
But my dearest child; how could it be;
you tried to take this gift I gave.
Just for a cry out; wishing to be safe.

My dear; you are safe, within yourself.
Just look deeper than ever before–
don't look back, the past is on the top shelf.
What you're looking for is far beyond the floor.

It's not gravel; or dirt.
Nothing of the sort.
Look further; and you will see.
That troubles that have been puzzling thee.

Satan Himself has loosened my grasp.
Get out now; and kick him fast.
Attack the man while he's down;
Will make happy. You shall see no frown.

Good Fight

Never fail to know the truth;
have hope in you; and in God; faith.
Be loved and resolute with.

Be strong, and forever be firm in your belief,
Carry on your praise, and never leave;
the side of God. beneath his right hand,
is the home; and place where you firmly stand.

Don't doubt, the undoubtedly.
Don't dislike, the lovingly.
Don't deter, the almighty.

Faith has you: Now be with it.
Fight, the Good fight;
with all your might.
Be strong; for God–
he said "THIS IS RIGHT!"

Got Back

I find it funny when your Jokes go down the drain.
I find them diabolically insane,
Your entire conscience is a shame.
And I laugh when you have no-one to blame.

Irony is a pitiful sin.
Your humour so cold;
It's only good for the bin.
You're the new toy; yet so old.

Sitting on the wall like a spare can.
You'll be lucky if you even have one fan.
Don't get me wrong; you're irreplaceable;
but your jokes make me so shakeable.

You remind me of the time;
when I stood at the end of the line,
this kid so shivered with fear;
Gently quivered his extra tear.

Bullied and tampered with; you're a mess.
With any friends; you'd be lucky to impress.
Standing at the back of the crowd.
Because being at the front is way too loud.

You're a social disembodied wreck,
You'd be lucky; if they even gave a heck.
Sometimes at the end of school;
Where no-one's around,
to see you break the rule.
And to make it worse you were easily found.

The last guy anyone chose at soccer;
falling behind in class; you right sucker.
Parents laughed up in your face;
did this make you feel a big disgrace?

Only one person in your world; alone.
Time to stand up and grow a backbone.
Give them what they're only good for.
Prove to the world you were never a dull-bore.

Heavy Hearts

Go along without the need of fear,
Nothing can harm you;
not when God is here.

His love is Strong
He is the endurance
His heavy heart is never Wrong;
and for that the angels dance.

God is rightful, and true
he wears his armour,
for me; and for you
we can stand as his toy soldier.

God will decide the fate
his move, like a chess piece
his opponent: Satan, with no defeat.

All who has been pranced upon;
The Devil's ill mannered drum,
Beats you until you're done.

Never shall you wear his crest;
for it is the Lord–Our God.
Who wears and reign's to be the best.
Remove your ill-fated honours
For God, promised us.
And with God's promise,
He endures forever.

I Can Be Free

Freedom? What is freedom?
Is freedom: to fly?
Is freedom: to die?
Is freedom: to forget?

Freedom? What is freedom?
Can freedom: be forever?
Can freedom: be never?
Is freedom: A lie?

No-one can truly be free.
Free to be, whatever;
you wanted to be-
Like a bird with glee;
fluttering up into the sky.

What if: you can be free.
What if: you can be;
who you wanted to be.
Would that be free?

To live free: would be away from rules.
To live free: would be life with no schools.
To be free: would be no need for money;
to be free: would be porridge with no honey.

I can be free: up; inside of my head.
I can be free: where rules are never read.
I can be free: If I really; honestly, wanted to.
I can be free: But I wouldn't know–what to do.

Judgement

You laugh and you haw;
bullet stricken upon thine paw.
Enlightened by awe.

As I sit and ponder on;
long and hard, I wander,
letting my curiosity arrive.

I gallivant on, into deep dimensions.
I still wonder, true peculiarity;
which of whom, holds the better mentions.

Not you, Nor I,
Not He, Nor She,
Not they, Nor We.
But Thee.

Thee of highest priests, thee of highest breaches.
He who bares judgement upon I, be only one.
The one whom he may be, is one who teaches;
with his love, and guidance, together be done.

The one I Speak of;
why it is, the LORD;
the Almighty One.

No-one but, God. Himself,
Bare a judge on me.
Your judgement be hasty,
where as his, tasty–
as a treat.

Love Endurance

My Love for you Is not forsaken.
My Love Endures forever;
and longs to be taken.
You will have me;
and we won't part–never.
This is my love which is for thee.

Hearts are throbbing
Which means something
how you make me laugh,
when you just do nothing.

My Love for you is ever growing
My Love for you is ever showing,
my Love for you is Never mourning.
Until that very next morning.

Love is a Battlefield

Love is a battlefield; of which we've grown.
Two sides so parallel; yet they're torn.
Definitive answers never told.
The questions we ask;
fill the weapons of which we hold.

Aimed; targeted and ready to blow.

Love is a battlefield; of which we've blown.
Two sides so Identical; yet never shown.
All the questions that buried inside;
Delve to the open, like a tide.

Love is a battlefield; where victory unfolds.
Two sides so powerful; yet one still holds;
The winner of the story; now be told.
And clarity of the case; now be sold.

Love was a battlefield; as you know.
Two sides so separate; as they go.
All the answers they have found;
Now there is peace within the sound.

Lover's Lost

Happy to tell you about my darling;
my first love.
He would be my Starling;
me his Dove.

We were always together;
Like the bird with her feather.
And it never was too cold;
And love never got to old.

Sitting on his bed.
Lifting tee-shirts over head.
We would hate for anything less,
now thinking back;
the break up: probably was for best.

So here I am alone;
thinking where this takes us;
With no one but my home.
You call this lust?

I never wanted, for anything to come from this.
And now I'm sitting, thinking of whom I miss.
Wishing for a moment where;
I could get one last kiss.
But that moment would never be there.

My Dog

Never have I but sought;
A dog, by lazy being what he is taught.
Amidst my sorrowful dismay.
curled spruce upon my bed;
This dog he must lay.

Never have I failed sought,
the golden lump had laid.
Barge the lump verbally, but what?
The dog just disobeyed.

So silent in his temper.
He lays with such beauty:
Comfort and joyed
Still like a picture: Polaroid.

Now the Dog, be unsettled
he jigs, doing "the stomp",
still; parallel with horizon,
He will lay, and wig' on.

My GOD

I found my GOD.
When I was at my lowest,
He took my hand; and he turned me around.
I said "Dear GOD; Oh GOD,
who hark heaven bound,
what do I do?"

With the roar of thunder, yet hollow;
as angelic; He be.
He answered "Alas; My Child, Now see.
Why do you seek suffering?
When you have talent, to Sing."

I thought could this be,
or is it dreams, of which I see.
I Have become a ray of Sunshine,
even when your skies are grey,
I smile from ear to ear, as My lord,
is with me, and forever will he stay.

So My friends, if like me,
You are accepted:
not even, into the bowels of Hell.
Look to the Lord Jesus,
he will, as my story will tell,
Help you out and get you through,
and turn your world the right way 'round.

My Sister, My Friend

Baring all thoughts, which I have.
I love you so much, as a child you are;
My sister, My friend, My key to a jovial Laugh.
We may be in the same house, but yet I feel so far.

My love for you, Sister, is rare
My heart for you I will rip and tear,
Just to show how much my love is there.
That's one thing you won't see again.

Today I may be here in loving Sight.
But with the way fate goes,
Tomorrow I could only be in your head at night.
Love and cherish my every breath
For we only get closer to Death.

Now the joyful part of this poem is; You.
I really wouldn't know what to do.
Without you, my key to ever after, would be none
I'm proud to say you're my sister even in our deepest burn.

Love you with all my Heart.

My Temptress Dismay (My Mistress)

Doth thou mistress sleep as thee, a mistress weep,
forsooth thee, a beautiful sound,
no hoarse grunt, no coarse compare.

for my mistress, golden is her hair.
down with thou, as thine temptress eyes,
Sought ye upon my domain.
out with thee and afar thou'st be carried.
by time and sun, be gone, what is to be remained?

My Mistress she fell, for one.
My Mistress' love was best to be undone.

Yet one doth not run, nor shall I slumber..
For if thy haste,
Be comparest upon ones breast to Summer,
to greet thee, to nurse thee and let us, now rake.
rewards are at best without risks to be take.

And yet thee protrude me, my hindrance;
doth thee by underestimation:
view me, amidst a chance..

No reward to be forced,
Will'st be a reward grossly missed.
You're temptress dismay doth not
foresee me as to your customs.

—Dedicated to a Dear friend: Corrienne Rowley.

Negative Hope

Tonight will be the night
the world loses sight,
the lights turn of and the day shuts down.

With the guns a blaze
Missiles launching
people in a daze.
Confusion becomes a pandemic, catastrophe.

The night's getting longer,
people suffering, and getting stronger.
No one will end the hellish endeavours.
It's down to us as a civilisation,
with our petrified shivers.

This is the day, the world ends.
Take the chance to love and forget,
to hold and protect,
the ones you truly love.
Your family and then your friends.

This is the day the world will sleep.
The power of Technology.
The lack of psychology,
this is the day, when we see our anatomy-
Flying like sky high.

Octroyed

Lead me for not into temptation; Lord
For you are the Power and the Glory,
  the eternal love in your kingdom—
this is what makes us: man of your world.

Do not, ever let us fall, fool to wrong.
Forever let us hold each other strong.
For it is your love, Lord—which will grow;
  and it is that love, which we need;
  only forever more; shall it really show!

God be strong and let us adore you;
God be Open and let us come too;
God be forever willing and never fail
God forever guide us with your trail,
  God never shall you, let us go.
God for it is you, that shall only know.

Which way the Satan's go we shall rejoice
  and tidy what was destroyed;
it will only be God and his almighty choice
  to bring us together as you octroyed.

One True Star

Life was amazing;
until you made me cry.
Sitting here gazing;
at that one star
Wondering what it be like;
to be up beyond the sky.
But that be too far.

Far for me to see.
Far from it all.

I want to be high;
so high I can touch the sky.
I want to be so close to you;
Now without you near-
I don't know what to do.
I still wish you were here.

But you are so far.
Sitting shining.
That one true star.

Only Holy

And holy, is your name
And holiness is what I aim;
I can't fulfill in myself
without what I really need.

You have planted the Seed;
I will nourish and help it grow.
Your name is all I need.

When I want to be contained
I come to you, and you leave me;
with no sins to be remained.

You make me holy.
And if I can return in favour
This is: if only!
I can't argue, you are my saviour.

This is all I say, that you make us holy.
Holy be us, and joined together.
Our love, never giving away;
and growing forever
this is all we have,
this is: if Only!

Personified

Brought to you, tied and chained-
Burnt by Satans remarkable
rules; I was maliciously detained.

A Spirit so unclean, with heavy Intensity.
Yet; there was sight, of extreme diversity.

Long live the true formidable,
The one who stands deity of them all.
Personified, and electrified;
and never defied.

Our FATHER, SON and SPIRIT.
Shall live; and live they Shall-
until eternity. And; then beyond.
OUR GOD SHALL NEVER FALL!

Pushed

When I'm gone;
you're on your own.
Bored and Cold–

You call him, and he drops it all.
Comes running to your demands.
All your problems in his hands.
But that is no where near it all.

Because when you are together.
Your time spent is almost forever.
What happened to me, making you feel special
In the vow I mentioned: "you're my angel."

Getting back to you soon;
I'd only wish you were over the moon–
but if it was down to you,
you'd have me set for the skies in a big balloon.

You just want him,
Well that is fine.
Take what you take;
But I won't be responsible for my actions.
And I will not take too good to a sanction.

Lock me up and throw away the key.
One of those Jackets; that'd look good on me.

Sometimes you make me cringe;
Going with "that" ridden rat–
Stabbed with a syringe;
every 2 hrs a hit..
Sounds to me like he's a dick.
But it's your choice, pick what you pick.

You knew what was best for you;
but your mind already knew–
what 'IT' wanted to do.

Questions of Worry

What does it mean;
when the zip tears the seam?
Tortured and scarred,
ripped and marred.

Is it the same;
when the water sinks the flame?
Burnt and Charred.
Frozen so hard.

So tell me now.
When I don't know how.
Is the answer nigh?
I need to know Why?

What does it mean;
when the bully is near defeat?
Battered and bruised.
Searched and cruised.

Why is it repeated;
every time I'm defeated?
Lost and lonesome.
Mundane or wholesome?

Reluctant Idiom of a Loser

Does one refrain from murder, with a pie?
Or do you indulge in slaughter through the eye.
Prolonged with the felicitous sigh.
Relieving the temptation, abundantly was nigh.

Only adults may read my hand,
the game of no winners;
but you can't read my Poker-face.
Just the hand of which I embrace.

Russian Roulette played by the sick.
Delivered unto us under the slick;
over-ruled by the idiom of a dick.
Never play with a cheetah,
because reluctantly he will beat ya.

Only you can understand,
the story of which this entailed,
no one is a winner,
so forever we have failed.

SALVATION!

The record kept playing;
as I kept praying,
the message was repeating;
as it lay a beating;
into my head.

Now, now and now; again it kept saying
and still I kept praying
the message carrying on, continuous.
A wave came over me, I felt Virtuous.

Once more the message bellowed from heaven
on the lasting day, the Sabbath, Number seven.
I took heed to this message and with it I repeat
"Now, is the day of God's favour;
Now, is the day of Salvation."
No longer does this message give me defeat.

I understand this message;
no longer do I fall hostage.

(In Inspiration from message of 2COR.6:2)

Small Dreams

I've always been a dreamer;
and it's great to finally appreciate them.
I've always jumped to the chance;
some would call me a prance.
But I can't hesitate the chance

Taking a grasp of life, with both hands.
Dedicating my all; in my ongoing demands,

I don't want to sound dull
but I've always been a modest guy;
Nothing gets me down.

I'm glad I feel so strong.
Otherwise life would be wrong,
My life dedicated to it all.
My dreams are growing;
But to be frank,
they are still very-very small.

That Will Be The Day

One fine day;
will be the day,
that you realise-
when we met
we linked eyes with eyes.

And on that day;
I'm sure you'll say,
What happened,
to what he had.
Did our love really get that bad.

But when you finish your recollection.
Just remember our love was not a selection.

You took what we had; and turned it to dust
You were so strong but still a lout for lust.
It will come with no Surprise;
you deserve all your cruel demise.

Please do understand
when you're cold and alone;
Shivering so cold;
gnawing your teeth down to the bone
I hope you grow old;
old and on your own . . .

That; Smells so Swell

Your perfume so sweet;
is an orgasm of nasal pleasure.
When the scent and nose meet,
my delights level to high pressure.

Berry beads; and Floral bud.
Really knocks me with a thud,
I get the highs from your smell;
when you walk by me, it really is swell.

Visually undertaken; your attitude tells,
But It's the perfume that smells.
Odour olfaction's
I just can't help my reactions.

The Arrival on the Caramel Sands

Forever you have been;
wrapped up in Satan's chains.
Will you feel the same;
if we ask you to change.

God forbids you from feeling low.
In his world of joy and heavenly glow;
it will be a giggle, That shall only show.

Bury your sins, and clap your hands;
God is coming, now clear the lands;
make a rigid path, and sound the bands.
God will arrive on caramel sands.

Through the seas, which he made passage.
Guiding along his fellowships.
Deeding to carry a message;
helping to clear people of their chips,

God is amazing, he has–
and will always work wonders.

The Journey

House abandoned, Left alone.
Frozen as the rain seeps through;
the rafters like a broken bone.

Just laying there,
in total fear
that you won't return here.

But yet I stay,
waiting upon that day,
when the coldness went away.

That was when I knew;
it had to be you.

The one which saved me from all my misery,
the one who changed my wintery;
into a dazzling sun-shining day.

God, has delivered me;
with the ability,
which, now I can see,
those that are visible
and which is beneath.

God, has told me
"you child, have much more to see."

The Toilet Paper which has Charisma

Isn't it lovely as I stick "à vous, derriere"
You wonder what to do here.
Isn't it lovely how as I dangle here
I could be out there,
burning as it may,
In the bright sun shining day,
with some horrific stanching air.
Isn't it lovely, how as you s*it;
I enjoy my moment as your saviour;
saving you from some horrifying mark,
scraped upon your brief's, dull and dark.
Isn't this lovely, as we sit together,
with this most favoured moment
yet you sit here, with no thanks.
I will remember that the next time we meet.
As I stick to your arse, you will thank God.
That, that was the last of me;
until you open the new role,
and again we sit, and repeat it all.

The Truth about Lies

Telling me this;
telling me that and it's all lies.
Stop; and just take a breath, before
your next lie; then watch your face-
as it hits the door.
You're a big disgrace.
You've gained nothing more.
Such a big mistake:
lying to me, mate!

But it's your life
so I'll let you live it-
with the consequences;
of your Bollocks
Crack the joke,
give us the kicks.

Whatever mate.
it's only your heart that may break.
Again, that was another Mistake.

The Wrong

A love so wrong;
yet your smile so strong.
A friendship made.
A life time displayed.

Time stood still;
but your face; was fulfill.
Could I take this;
it was a hit-or-miss.

I chanced it well
And in love I fell.
This woman; a friend.
This dearest; until the end.

So take me aback;
my love; was a heart-attack.
And in love it hurled
and this twisted my world.

Now I sit and choose?
Which one shall I lose?
A life-long friend;
or the love–that will never end . . .

Tongues

Because God came to me today,
and this, by truth is what he had to say.
"Child you come to me, with words unknown;
speak to me, even when words are not showing."

To that be known to me
where shall I start;
and words what will they be?
Truthfully it must be an art.

The power of tongues just flew away
Unknowing to me, what had I to say.
God Has anointed you, the power of tongues
Now worship God when words unknown.
And God will enlighten you with soulful songs.

God Speaks, and moves in mysterious ways
It is to me to observe as I go about my Days.

GOD BLESS

UNFAIRLY CONVICTED!

I may be guilty of conviction;
you can close my case down;
for all I've done is affection,
break me and rake me;
but I will never frown
Hurt me and desert me;
but I won't play the clown;
to your evil, sadistic game
I will weep no sound,
whatever it is that you aim-
to gain.

Do not try to tease;
what you cannot seize.
Do not alter anything;
for it is that way;
as is everything.

The only one, who bids me to question;
is He who created me, without an exception.
No-one will find humour in my defeat,
as I stand strong, firmly on my own feet.

Holding me tall, firm as I Stand
is the Rock of my Solidity,
he who holds me Hand-in-hand.
look at yourself, before you get slapped;
by what is the true reality.

Worthless

Don't make me promises that you cannot keep.
Always saying you're sorry;
really makes me weak . . .

But I won't say you're worth it.
I won't say you've tried.
I won't say you've earnt it.
I won't say you've tried.

So why do I give you my heart like that?
So why did I just give it? when now I want it back.
I know you're gonna leave me.
I know you wanna replace me.

But did I deserve it like that?

And; now I won't say you're worth it.
I won't say you've tried.
I won't say you've earnt it,
I won't say you've tried.
So why did you take it like that?

But I won't say you're worth it.
I won't say you've tried.
I won't say you've earnt it.
I won't say you've tried.

Billions of people In this world;
and you had to choose the most vulnerable.
I guess that's just how you roll.
Taking each one-by-one.
Do you ever think; for what you've done?

I won't say you're worth it.
I won't say you've tried.
I won't say you've earnt it.
I won't say you've tried.
So why'd you take it like that?

Deceit at Its Best

No one will suspect.
They only see what they expect,
nothing more nor anything less
this is deceit at its best.

We see rain-clouds so expect rain;
Never the thunder which groans,
or the lightning that follows.

Standing drenched by rain,
Feeling inside, this deep shame.
Thinking how to prevent this:
I'll never leave the house,
Without a coat again.

Like a child on a tantrum;
the heavens explode,
the rain unfolds;
a burst of exasperation
a bright light. No exaggeration.

And again the thunder rolls!

Dreadful Eyes

Closed tight the dreams are clear.
Wide open and nothing is here.
Where's the understanding in that?

Vision so acceptable;
I appreciate it very much.
But what is a vision?
without light, as such?
Do I make an honest decision;
and sit this one out.
Where's the logic in that?

Trusted eyes, my friendly eyes.
Helpful eyes.
DREADFUL EYES!

Failing to provide me;
with the constant need.
An Elusive feed.
Where's the Loyalty In that?

-

Irish Luck

Can't you see what you may make?
I'm dying here without ya!
Cracking from the heartache;
The burden; left behind.

They said to me; He's just a waste of your time.
Don't get involved; or, Never mind.
But my curious heart loves to wander.
Yet you walked out on me;
now I sit here and I wonder

The time we spent apart;
will make our love grow stronger
But in fact it hurts so much;
I can't take it any longer.
Yet that's what I get for listening to you.

This must be Irish Luck;
for a total piece of Muck.

Don't get me wrong;
you're a decent bloke.
But clearly you're headstrong;
and your heart's a joke.

Pack up and leave,
why should I waste my time.
If you never wanted me;
then you could've just said–
but of course you know best!
Forget his feeling, just mess with his head.
I'll make sure you don't do it to the rest.

Seductive, Sensuous.

There's a glint in your eye,
as I sit and watch you cry.
I don't want to hurt you like this,
Just turn around-
After this one last kiss.

As you walk away;
you fall to the ground.
I know this is the way-
to comfort you with no sound.
But How can I leave;
and How can I hold you anyway!
If you want it now,
Tell me to stay!!!
Before I go.

If I go, I won't know,
How you really felt.
Holding me to your sensuous body
Seductively lured; my nerves melt.

I can't leave you like this,
Not wondering now, what I will miss.
This dreamy fantasy-
Will soon be my ultimate, Reality!
Eventually reaching a casualty.

The Best Contender

My Head ain't hot;
I'm just taking my best shot-
at being what you cannot.

Don't get me wrong;
It is good what you've done,
yet we all know I can do better!

Hit me with your best;
you can't penetrate-
my bullet proof vest.
I Love how you hate.

Attack me harder,
I still will use this armour.
Kick me when I'm down;
rip the honourees of my crown,

I'm still the best in my mind.
A better contender-
I still need to find.
take what you can and surrender.

I am simply the best;
totally better than the rest,
So give up while the road's ahead.
Or you'll miss the end,
and flip into a pool of red.

The Lion

Sunshine bursts from the lion's eyes.
Coarse golden shining bright;
Strong and fierce; proud with might.
Laughing at everyone's demise.

So Credited and feared by all,
The Lion that's not so small.
See the Lion; so heavy and bold,
Not only a terrifying creature.
But built with gracious structure.

His appetite so delicately planned,
as he stalks his prey; playing in the sand.
Humorous to him, but horrific from them,
A nice bit of boar, would make excellent ham.

This beast of eccentricity.
Pounces quick, It's electricity!
No one knows when he'll pounce.
A swipe by his paw across the face—
you will definitely bounce.
You will be failing his grace.

Resistance by this animal? Be it futile.
Elegantly dancing, mocking you in style,
Designed to flaunt—all that he has;
He'll eat you up, and gobble you fast.

The Practicality of Living Life

You can't choose Life; but you can
listen to those that are judicious,
Judge you with good Quality-
An aura so delicious;
The taste is almost sickly.

Choosing your friends,
is the best way to fill in the end-
A big grasping hold;
on a story untold.

Be practical; take care in your work.
Watch for the one that hates
they will do anything, even stab you–
but the one that's always there;
they know what to do.
They're your true mates.
Wherever you are they are there.

This is the good judgement;
Of a brilliant mate.
Great mate's are the practicality
In your living reality.

www.ingramcontent.com/pod-product-compliance
Ingram Content Group UK Ltd.
Pitfield, Milton Keynes, MK11 3LW, UK
UKHW040335101125
8849UKWH00041B/565